The
Faith in
Action
Series

A Powerful Voice

The Story of Bono
from U2

Deborah Helme

Illustrated by Brian Platt

RMEP

RELIGIOUS AND MORAL EDUCATION PRESS

A POWERFUL VOICE

The Story of Bono from U2

The noise of the crowd filled every inch of the stadium. The shouts, stamping and screaming seemed to fuse together to make an impossible roar. Towards the front of the stage it was possible to make out eager expressions as desperate fans waited impatiently for the music. Yet just behind those at the front, the crowd began to merge. Towards the middle it was hard to separate the mass of people from each other, and as the crowd stretched back it was hard to define its end. Even the venue itself seemed to blur, at first it seemed like a large night-club, then changing into a concert hall, until it felt more like an outdoor sports stadium.

The lights went out and for a fraction of a second the roar seemed to silence in anticipation, then the lights flicked on again full glare and the roar reached deafening point. For a moment the men on stage froze, as though overcome with the scale of the occasion and then with a fast count-in the band began.

The roaring crowd became a mesmerised mass of appreciative supporters, applauding, singing and clapping. The adrenaline rush felt by the band seemed to be reaching the fans too. Suddenly the lead singer, Paul Hewson, began to sing *Gloria*, praising his God. A glint of amazement appeared in his eyes as the crowd seemed to love the song and began to sing along. Was it possible?

Paul Hewson, known to the world as Bono, is the lead singer of the band U2 and has enjoyed long and sustained success in the music industry. The band was formed when he was still at school and he may have dreamt like this of being famous one day. Yet maybe even he didn't imagine they would be so successful. The band's music has been at the top of singles and album charts all around the world. They have won numerous Grammy Awards and the Brit Award for 'Outstanding Contribution to Music'.

Yet Bono has not only received international acclaim for his music. He is also acknowledged to be a tireless and ardent campaigner for a better and fairer world. Although he is reluctant to talk about God, Bono's faith and his desire to see a better world have motivated many of his actions.

Starting Out

One day during the autumn of 1976, Paul glanced over the school notice-board – it was a good way of finding out if anything interesting was happening in or around the school. He was about to walk away when he noticed a new advert about being in a band. Paul liked music, he played guitar and thought one day it could make him famous. He decided to find out more.

He arrived at the first meeting of the band and was surprised to find that only a few others had turned up. He wasn't shy and soon took part in the discussions on what kind of band they should be. Before long he was almost in charge of the discussion, he seemed to be a natural leader. Paul was disappointed to discover that three of the five boys serious about the group could play the guitar better than he could. There was no way they needed so many guitarists – he'd have to find a different role. He had a decent voice and had already written some songs, so he ended up being vocalist and song-writer. The advert had been put up by Larry Mullen, who played the drums. Adam Clayton played bass guitar and the other two guitarists were brothers – David and Dick Evans. When the band started, Larry and David were only 14, Paul and Adam had just turned 16, Dick was slightly older.

The boys all shared an intense ambition to succeed, but it took them a while to discover an identity for themselves. The influences on the band were diverse, they included the Beatles, the Rolling Stones, Bruce Springsteen and, contemporary to them at that time, punk. Although they didn't want to be a punk band they were inspired by the way bands like The Ramones and The Clash sang with such raw attitude.

U2's Website

To find out more about the band and their music, you could visit the U2 website at www.U2.com

They began by attempting to do cover versions of songs but their small audiences hated it – they needed original material. Combining rhythm, guitar skills, a flair for song-writing and plenty of practice, the band gradually began to create its own unique sound and appeal.

At first they called the band 'Feedback' and then 'The Hype' until they finally settled on 'U2'. The name came from a special type of American reconnaissance spy aircraft that was shot down in Russia around the time Paul was born. It also immediately involved the fans, 'you too'. The boys gave each other nicknames as well. The guitarist David Evans was called 'The Edge' and Paul was called 'Bono Vox' (meaning 'good voice'), which some of his friends had seen written on a poster. The nickname became shortened to just 'Bono' and at first he hated it, but it stuck.

Whenever Bono wrote songs, he had to write about things that mattered to him. His approach to writing was unusual – sometimes he'd wait until the last possible moment and then write the words down in a rush. He was a confident colourful character and enjoyed drama and 'being up front'. He was sociable and spent little time at home. His mother had died suddenly when he was 14 and he lived with his father – his older brother had already left home. The tragedy of losing his mother so young had a big impact on Bono. It wasn't an easy childhood, yet from the beginning he had confidence and believed the band would succeed.

What Do You Think?

Important: In answering 'What Do You Think?' questions in this book, it is important that you not only state your opinion but also give as many reasons as possible for your opinion.

1. Bono and U2 worked hard to get the sound of their music right. Why do you think they kept going? What helps you to keep going when you set your mind to something?

2. Even when he was still at school, Bono wrote about things that mattered to him. What current events or issues make you feel strongly? If Bono was at school writing today, what do you think he would be writing about?

3. How would you describe Bono's attitude to life at this stage? How would you describe your attitude to life?

Faith or Fame?

Bono grew up in Dublin. It was a bustling city like many others, but one thing that perhaps made it a little different was that everyone was very aware of their family background. Most people were either Roman Catholic or Protestant. This affected much more than where they went to church, it decided who they mixed with and even which school they went to. Bono was unusual from the start because his mother was Protestant and his father was Roman Catholic.

He attended Mount Temple Comprehensive School. This was the Irish Republic's first school for both Protestants and Catholics and the students were taught together. The school was a real experiment. The effect of not separating Protestants and Catholics might have been to delete religion from the agenda altogether. Yet Christianity seemed to gather momentum in the school at that time. There were regular meetings for prayer and students all through the school started getting together to talk about God.

Bono found a faith at this time. He thought it was radical that the God who created the universe might be interested in him. Formal religion didn't appeal to him, perhaps he had seen too much of the damage that different religious organisations had done to his country and his family – yet following the example of Jesus did appeal. He joined in the school meetings and started going to a Christian group called the 'Shalom Community', whose meetings were far more informal than the traditional Catholic and Protestant styles of worship. Larry and The Edge went with him.

At the same time Bono also belonged to a gang called 'Lypton Village'. It was a group of friends who liked to think creatively and radically. They also provided an audience for the band to try out some of its material. Occasionally Bono ran into trouble on the streets of Dublin. Although he could look after himself, he didn't like fighting and tried to avoid it.

Bono's band, faith and gang were all very important to him and all had an influence on him. He kept busy and a lot of his time was spent practising with the group. They began to play local pubs and clubs and eventually felt confident enough to enter a talent competition. They were amazed to win it and went on to record a demo, but it didn't work out as well as they had hoped and things seemed to go back to normal. In 1978, Dick Evans left the band to

Bono and Ali at a party before the 2003 Oscar awards

Photo by Matt Baron/BEI/Rex Features

study engineering at Dublin's Trinity College but U2 continued undaunted. After they won the talent competition, Adam had managed to persuade a music journalist, Bill Graham, to see them play. He was impressed by the band and throughout his life remained a supporter and ally. He put them in touch with a manager who agreed to take U2 on. Finally they were beginning to get somewhere but progress was slow.

Despite this frustration U2's ambition never disappeared, and when they left school they were still determined to be rock stars. To finance the band Bono worked part time in a petrol station. His life continued to be full of music and his faith.

Step by step, the band played bigger gigs, got a recording contract and became better known in Ireland. They released their first album, *Boy*, in 1980. Their excitement and enthusiasm grew and all seemed to be going just as they had dreamed, but then they hit a problem. Their second album, *October*, included songs with strong spiritual themes, like *Gloria* and *Rejoice*, yet despite this it received good reviews from the music industry, which didn't generally react well to religious bands or lyrics. Surprisingly though, the response they received from the Shalom

Community was not so positive. Some people in the Christian group were not convinced that it would be good for U2 to continue. They were concerned that the young men, now aged 19–20, would not cope well with all the temptations that being successful rock stars would bring, like drugs, sex and materialism. Bono, Larry and The Edge were devastated. They didn't want to give up the band or the Shalom Community.

They struggled for a long time with what they felt would be the right thing to do. In the end they decided to leave the Shalom Community but not to leave God. In fact for Bono it was more rebellious to read the Bible on tour than to do drugs. He said, 'Rebellion starts at home, in your heart, in your refusal to compromise your beliefs and values.' Bono has never been able to be an ordinary member of a church since he has been famous, yet the importance of his faith is reflected in many of his songs.

Throughout this time Bono had been in love. His girlfriend, Alison (Ali) Stewart, was the same age as him and they had been at school together. The first time he had tried to impress her and ask her out she had not been interested, but he hadn't given up and had spent years pursuing her. Finally, when he was 17, she changed her mind. She was a strong independent person and was never prepared simply to live in Bono's shadow. Despite the pressures on them both, they stayed together and in August 1982, just as Bono began to become really famous, they amazed the world by getting married. Bono was then only 22 years old. He and Ali have now been married for over 20 years and have four children. The family still lives in the Republic of Ireland.

What Do You Think?

1. God appealed to Bono but 'formal' religion' didn't. Formal or institutional religion still doesn't appeal to many young people today. Why do you think 'the God who created the universe' interested Bono but the traditions of the Church didn't? What do you think the difference is?

2. In what ways might it be difficult for a celebrity to have or express a faith?

3. Bono made big decisions about his beliefs and values when he was a teenager. He was influenced by the Christian faith. What influences your beliefs and values? You may want to think about the following areas: family, friends, media, music, etc.

4. **On the U2 website at www.U2.com** look at the lyrics to the song *Gloria*. Can you find any suggestion of a stutter in the lyrics? Why do you think Bono wrote the song like that? What do you think he was expressing in the words 'But only in you I'm complete'?

Sunday Bloody Sunday

Somewhere in the Irish Republic people were making bombs for the IRA (Irish Republican Army), somewhere in Northern Ireland people were acting as British informers. People both south and north of the border felt passionately enough to kill or be killed to create or prevent a united Ireland. Undoubtedly one of the areas to have suffered much from these troubles was Belfast, so it is no coincidence that it was there that U2 decided to introduce to the world one of their most controversial songs.

They were in Maysfield Hall in Belfast just before Christmas in 1982. They were playing to thousands of fans in a sell-out crowd and the atmosphere was electric. All of a sudden the mood changed as Bono introduced the new song. He explained it was about Northern Ireland, but it wasn't a 'rebel' song and if the crowd didn't like it then they would never play it in Belfast again. There was a pause, Larry began on the drums and Bono sang, 'I can't believe the news today ... Sunday Bloody Sunday ... '

It was an amazingly brave song. Here was an Irish band playing a Northern Irish audience about the problems of their divided country, problems which would have saturated and affected everyone's lives so profoundly. They weren't intending to further the cause of either side, they were simply asking the question 'How long?' How long would it all go on for? When was all the fighting and suffering going to end? *Sunday Bloody Sunday* asked the questions, it didn't give any answers. At the end of the song the crowd cheered.

The fighting and unrest in Ireland go back for centuries. In modern times, the conflict has been essentially between the Republicans, those – primarily Catholics – who wish to have a unified Ireland and no interference from the British government, and the Loyalists – primarily Protestants – who would like to remain a part of the United Kingdom. For hundreds of years the problems have bubbled away, often flaring up in violent clashes and battles. A political solution to the problem was attempted in 1921, when the country was divided into two. The southern part of Ireland became the

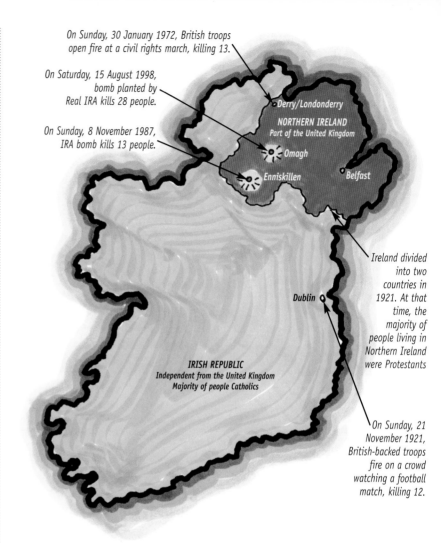

On Sunday, 30 January 1972, British troops open fire at a civil rights march, killing 13.

On Saturday, 15 August 1998, bomb planted by Real IRA kills 28 people.

On Sunday, 8 November 1987, IRA bomb kills 13 people.

Derry/Londonderry

NORTHERN IRELAND
Part of the United Kingdom

Omagh

Enniskillen

Belfast

Ireland divided into two countries in 1921. At that time, the majority of people living in Northern Ireland were Protestants

Dublin

IRISH REPUBLIC
Independent from the United Kingdom
Majority of people Catholics

On Sunday, 21 November 1921, British-backed troops fire on a crowd watching a football match, killing 12.

Irish Republic and independent from the United Kingdom, whilst Northern Ireland remained part of the UK and under the UK government. The majority of those in the Irish Republic were Catholic and the majority of those in Northern Ireland were Protestant, but huge problems remained for the Catholic minority in Northern Ireland. The clashes and violence continue to this day. However, it is only small groups of people from each side of the conflict who choose to use violence to resolve the problems. The majority of people would prefer to find a peaceful solution.

Sunday Bloody Sunday refers to two important dates in these clashes and troubles. One is Sunday, 21 November 1921, when following the murder of fourteen British agents, British-backed troops retaliated by indiscriminately killing twelve unarmed people who were watching a football match in Croke Park, Dublin (a venue U2 later played). The other 'Bloody Sunday' was 30 January 1972, when British troops opened fire at a civil rights march in Derry/Londonderry, killing thirteen Catholics. Although these two tragic events in Irish history involved British shootings, the song was not intended to be seen as supporting the IRA, who strongly opposed British rule in Northern Ireland. Whenever it was sung live, Bono specifically explained it wasn't a 'rebel' song, instead it spoke out against violence.

Using a song to cry out against the pain caused by this political situation could have destroyed U2's career before it had properly taken off. Yet this chance to protest was too important an opportunity for them to miss. It had been The Edge's idea to write something about the conflict in Northern Ireland

Notes on the Lyrics of *Sunday Bloody Sunday*

'battle call' (line 7) – Some people see the conflict in Northern Ireland as a war with each side calling supporters to battle. Bono seems to be saying he doesn't want to be forced to take a side.

'... the victory Jesus won, On a Sunday ...' (last verse) – Jesus was crucified on a Friday and Christians believe he was resurrected (came back to life) on the Sunday. Christians remember this on Easter Sunday, especially, but every Sunday is special to Christians.

Christians also believe that through his death and resurrection, Jesus won the battle against evil and death.

and to link it somehow to the death and resurrection of Jesus. The Edge wrote the music and Bono agonised over writing the lyrics.

Sunday Bloody Sunday became a great favourite with U2's fans and had a huge impact, especially on live audiences. Then on Remembrance Sunday, 8 November 1987, nearly five years after they first played it, the IRA exploded a bomb at a war memorial in Enniskillen killing thirteen innocent people. That night U2 were giving a concert in Denver, USA. Never before had the lines from *Sunday Bloody Sunday* 'I can't believe the news today/I can't close my eyes and make it go away' seemed so appropriate. After that night the band didn't play it again live for almost ten years.

For many *Sunday Bloody Sunday* was the first song that made it clear that U2 were interested in politics. They continued to write and sing about all kinds of issues throughout the world that frustrated them. But that didn't lessen their concern for the problems in Northern Ireland.

In 1998, sixteen years after they'd first sung *Sunday Bloody Sunday* in Belfast, Bono and the other band members had an opportunity to play a small direct part in the efforts for peace. Politicians were attempting to start bringing lasting peace to Northern Ireland through the Good Friday Agreement. This would

Photo by Martin McCullough/Rex Features

Bono with David Trimble (left) and John Hume (right) at the vote 'Yes' rock gig in 1998

establish a governing body which would include leaders from each side of the dispute. There was to be a joint referendum (vote) in Northern Ireland and the Irish Republic about whether or not to implement (put into effect) the Agreement. The 'vote-yes' campaign had wide support both in Northern Ireland and internationally, including the backing of Nelson Mandela, President of South Africa, and Bill Clinton, President of the USA. It was also supported by the leaders of two major political parties in Northern Ireland, the Ulster Unionist Party leader David Trimble and the SDLP leader John Hume. To mobilise the 'Yes' youth vote, a rock gig was organised. All the members of U2 were there and arguably the highlight of the event was when Bono invited John Hume and David Trimble onto the stage. He stood between them and held up their arms in a salute of hope. The 'Yes' vote won the referendum and Northern Ireland took a small step nearer to lasting peace with Bono and U2 having made a tiny contribution.

Despite the hope that the Good Friday Agreement brought, Northern Ireland has not yet found a complete lasting peace. One horrific reminder of this was the bombing by the Real IRA (a breakaway group) in Omagh. On Saturday, 15 August 1998 a terrorist car-bomb went off in Omagh's town centre killing twenty-eight people and injuring hundreds. In response to this, in the song *Peace on Earth* Bono wrote, 'No-one cries like a mother cries/For peace on Earth'. For twenty years he had been crying out with the same message against violence.

What Do You Think?

1. Do you think superstars should get involved with politics? Was Bono wise, brave or foolish to write and sing about the problems in Northern Ireland? Explain your reasons.

2. Bono wanted to encourage young people to vote 'Yes' for the Good Friday Agreement. Why do you think young people might not have voted, even if they agreed with the Good Friday Agreement? Why might a young person have voted 'No'? Do you think voting in political matters or elections is important? What kind of issues would be important enough to make you want to vote?

3. **On the U2 website at www.U2.com** look at the lyrics of *Sunday Bloody Sunday*. What you think Bono is saying? (You may find the notes on page 9 helpful.) Do you think the song could apply to other conflicts in different parts of the world? Give reasons for your answer.

Passion for Justice

Bono felt strongly about the well-being of the people in Northern Ireland and the Irish Republic, but his concern for peace, justice and a fairer world includes many other nations and issues. When he supports a cause, he doesn't take a vague interest in it as a celebrity. He gets to know the issues in great detail, he lives and breathes the problems, he visits, questions, reads, investigates and then he responds.

The desperation of the people starving in Ethiopia during the famine of 1985 was viewed in horror in the West. The developed world could not escape the television pictures of tiny children with huge extended stomachs, endlessly brushing away flies from their infected mouths and eyes. The pictures were harrowing, but to be there and see the suffering must have been much worse. Yet Bono and his wife Ali decided to go to Ethiopia themselves and help in any practical way they could. Bono and U2 had already responded to the disaster by taking part in Live Aid. This was a fund-raising concert broadcast around the

Bono performing at Live Aid in 1985

Photo by Rex Features

world and had raised 200 million dollars to support famine relief. Helping to raise this money was not enough for Bono and, determined to find out more about the problems, he went with Ali to a refugee camp for a month.

Despite their growing fortune and fame, they demanded no special treatment, getting involved in the everyday tasks, even rolling up their sleeves and shovelling dirt when necessary. Their responsibilities included working at a feeding station which had to be fenced in and guarded to protect the food and medical supplies. They worked alongside aid workers who had to make horrifying life and death decisions over who should be helped, or not. To Bono and Ali some of the starving Ethiopians stopped being statistics and became real people, with real families, feelings and dreams. Perhaps it was there that political injustice stopped being a concern to Bono and instead became a passion.

During the 1980s Bono's humanitarian efforts were numerous. For example, he worked closely with the human-rights charity Amnesty International, highlighting some of their different campaigns on U2 albums. In 1986 he and Ali went with Amnesty International on a fact-finding tour of El Salvador. At the time the government in El Salvador, backed by the USA, was fighting a civil war with a socialist opposition group. Bono and Ali arrived at the capital San Salvador at the height of the fighting and on their way from the airport to a nearby village, the village came under attack. Bono desperately looked for cover as the planes flew over dropping bombs. Later on in their trip, troops threatened them by firing machine-guns over their heads. In response Bono wrote the song *Bullet the Blue Sky*, which criticised outside involvement in this conflict. He had enjoyed huge success in the USA, yet he wasn't afraid to sing against their foreign policies when he thought they were wrong. He wasn't prepared to sacrifice his integrity.

Bullet the Blue Sky is on the album *The Joshua Tree*, an album which reflects the wide range of Bono's interests and concerns. For example, *Mother of the Disappeared* refers to the horrors of General Pinochet's Argentina, where thousands of people unsympathetic to his government 'disappeared' and were never seen again. *Red Hill Mining Town* is about the struggles of the British miners' strike, *Running to Stand Still* is concerned with the drug problems in Dublin's Ballymun.

Perhaps it is no surprise that Bono's critics complained that he shouldn't take on all the world's problems. How could such a rich rock star relate to the poor and suffering? Bono was a confident character who could stand up and sing up against criticism, yet eventually these comments did start to get through to him. He had been honest, he had told the world what he thought, everyone seemed to know all about him. Maybe he now felt overexposed and vulnerable.

What Do You Think?

1. Why do you think Bono wanted to go to Ethiopia himself when he had already helped to raise so much money for the people there? If you had the opportunity, would you go to visit a developing country? What do you think you would find (a) most difficult and (b) most informative there?

2. During his visit to El Salvador Bono was in grave danger. Do you think this experience put him off travelling in the future or made him even more determined to become involved in international politics? Would fear or intimidation stop you from doing something you believed in? When might you persevere? Give examples.

No More Mr Nice Guy

Musically, Bono had achieved many things rock singers must dream of. He had travelled the world and he had a massive fan following. Everywhere he went people recognised him. When he said something, people wrote it down and printed it. He was a big celebrity.

On 31 December 1989, U2 played the last of four sell-out gigs in Dublin. At the end of the concert Bono announced that the band was going to go and 'dream it up all over again'. They didn't tour or release any new music for two years. During that time they did record a new album but it was completely different to anything they had done before.

First they released the single *The Fly*. It was a new kind of music for the band, with distorted vocals and a dark restlessness. It prepared their fans for the new style of U2 music in the album *Achtung Baby*. Not only was the music different but so was Bono. During the two-year

Photo by Andre Csillag/Rex Features

world-wide Zoo TV/Zooropa tour Bono began to wear big dark goggles. These wrapped around his face making it impossible to see his eyes and made him look a little like a fly. He wore tight black leather and his behaviour was different; he was arrogant and rarely serious. He acted like this on and off the stage. He had made himself into an act, a character, a persona – almost another person. His critics and even some of his fans weren't completely sure what was going on. Had he changed or was he acting? He had another character, Mirrorball Man, who wore gold, was very vain, even looking into a large mirror on stage. As the tour continued a third character developed: MacPhisto, who was a little like a horn-wearing devil.

Bono didn't step out of character to explain what he was doing, but he did send out some clues. For example, in a video to go with the song *Hold Me, Thrill Me, Kiss Me, Kill Me* there is a glimpse of a book called *The Screwtape Letters*, by C. S. Lewis.

This book begins with quotes about mocking the devil – maybe that was what Bono was trying to do.

During the same tour U2 also surprised their fans and the music industry with extremely elaborate stage sets. Dominating the stage were 36 television screens flashing up different pictures or messages. The idea for the TV screens had been prompted by the Gulf War in the early 1990s. From the comfort and security of their front rooms people had been able to watch bombs hitting targets and killing real people, yet by pressing their remote controls they could switch to a cartoon. In a similar way, the stage-set screens flashed up provocative, contrasting images and slogans or words like 'Believe', 'Celebrity is joy', 'Mock the Devil', 'Everything you know is wrong'. Fans and critics alike were allowed to decide for themselves what the U2 television screens were all about.

Yet the actual lyrics of these new songs U2 were singing were also a clue to what was happening in the minds and life journeys of Bono and the other band members. There was an honesty in the lyrics: they sang about doubts,

Bono on stage as MacPhisto

Photo by Brian Rasic/Rex Features

What Do You Think?

1. During this phase of his career Bono was accused of being very cynical. How would you describe 'cynical'? Do you think he was? Are you ever cynical? What makes you feel that way?

2. Bono's beliefs shape his life, but he also admits to having doubts. Can faith and doubt go hand in hand? Give reasons for your answer.

3. Imagine you are a fan of U2. During this time you have the chance to ask Bono, 'What's up?' What do you think he would have said?

disappointments and frustrations. In fact many of the songs on *Achtung Baby* were influenced by the break-up of The Edge's marriage. In the chart-topping single *The Fly* there even seems to be a debate in the chorus contrasting humans and God, good and evil. There is a search for the truth, for meaning and for God that is echoed in many of the songs written by Bono.

Sing a New Song

Many of U2's concerts in the 1980s ended with the song *40*. Fans knew the lyrics and would immediately sing along, 'I will sing, sing a new song ...' . It was a song based on Psalm 40 from the Bible – the kind of song that people would usually sing in a religious service rather than a pop concert.

From the age of twelve Bono was fascinated by the Psalms and King David, the powerful Jewish leader who is accredited with writing many of them. David was successful and believed in God yet he didn't lead a perfect life. He seduced someone else's wife and then arranged for her husband to be killed. In the Psalms, David cries out to God to help him with his failures and mistakes as well as thanking God for his successes. Bono was asked to write an introduction to the Psalms for a special publication of the Bible. He wrote: 'For me, it's in his despair that the Psalmist [Psalm writer] really reveals the nature of his special relationship with God. Honesty, even to the point of anger ...' .

The simplest definition of a psalm is a sacred or religious

song or hymn. Therefore many of Bono's songs could be described as psalms. In them, just like King David thousands of years ago, Bono reveals the nature of his special relationship with God, he is honest even to the point of anger. For example in the song *Peace on Earth*, written after the Omagh bombing, Bono complains that the words 'peace on earth' are getting stuck in his throat. 'Peace on earth' was part of the angels' message at the birth of Jesus, but in this song Bono seems to feel that Jesus wasn't doing much to bring peace to the people of Omagh in 1998.

Bono felt the tension that many believers feel between a loving, powerful God and the suffering and injustices in the world. This did not lead him to abandon all his beliefs but it drove him to question God and to try to reduce some of the suffering. Perhaps as he lobbied politicians when he felt strongly about injustice, he also lobbied God when things didn't seem to be going to plan.

At the end of the album *Pop*, there is a song written for the end of the Millennium, when so much of society seemed to have rejected belief in God. The song entitled *Wake Up Dead Man* calls for God and Jesus to reveal themselves. 'This is the end of the century when God is supposed to be dead,' Bono said. 'People want to believe but they're angry. If God's not dead there's some questions we want to ask him.' (*U2 Into the Heart*, by Niall Stokes, Thunder Mouth Press, 1996)

In the following album, *All That You Can't Leave Behind*, Bono's song-writing seems less harsh. In the song *Grace* he seems less angry about what God hasn't done and more amazed by what he believes God has done. 'Grace' can be a girl's name but it is also a word used by Christians when they talk about God's love and action in the world. In the song, Bono describes 'Grace' as a beautiful woman who finds beauty in everything and can make ugly things beautiful. It is a song that celebrates the good instead of focusing on the bad.

Notes on the Lyrics of *Grace*

'Grace' is a word used by Christians to describe God's love and action in the world. Christians believe that God doesn't wait for humanity to be beautiful and loveable, instead God freely gives his undeserved love, and that love then makes humanity beautiful and loveable.

'Removes the stain' (line 3) – This may refer to the Bible verse Isaiah 1:18: '... You are stained red with sin, but I [God] will wash you as clean as snow ...' (*Good News Bible*).

'karma' (verse 3) – This word means 'action' and is used to describe Hindu or Buddhist beliefs concerning how someone's present life and actions affect their next reincarnation (rebirth).

What Do You Think?

1. If you could lobby (pester) God about something you didn't like in the world, what would you choose?

2. Do you think it's right to express anger to God? Does your answer depend on whether the person expressing anger is religious or not? Give reasons for your answer.

A Stone in the President's Shoe

Following his experiences in Ethiopia, Bono continued to try to help the plight of the poor in Africa. Fifteen years after Live Aid he was asked to support the Jubilee 2000 campaign. The idea of Jubilee 2000 was to celebrate the New Millennium in a positive way through the cancellation of Third World debt. Several decades earlier many poor countries or 'Third World' countries had been encouraged to borrow money from richer ones. The world economic climate then changed and these poorer countries found they had to pay back not just the loans but also unexpected and ever-increasing interest. This meant that they had to divert the scarce funds they had from clean water, education and health, etc., into debt repayment.

Jubilee 2000 was an interfaith campaign, inspired by words from Leviticus, a book in the Hebrew Bible/Christian Old Testament. This book contains rules for living. It states that every fifty years there should be a special Jubilee year when debts are cancelled and everyone should have the chance to make a new economic start. This seemed a perfect solution for the Third World countries stuck in the endless spiral of debt repayment; a really special way to celebrate the New Millennium.

The campaign was managed from the offices of Christian Aid and they invited Bono to help catch the attention of the media. In the end his contribution was far greater than that. He was campaigning for a cause he felt passionate about and as well as attracting media interest he also proved himself a brilliant lobbyist for the cause. He researched, read and impressed economic experts and world leaders with the level of his knowledge and understanding of the problems and issues faced. He travelled extensively on behalf of the campaign, speaking to many influential world leaders and politicians. He even met the Pope, who gave him a rosary. In return Bono handed him one of his pairs of famous wrap-round dark glasses, which the Pope immediately wore. Bono spoke to the British Prime Minister, the

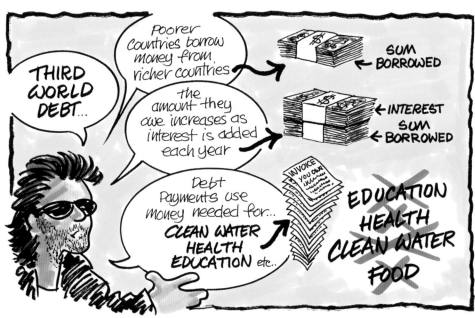

American President and addressed the assembly of the United Nations.

Not all the hopes of the Jubilee 2000 campaign were realised but it did make a huge impact. By the end of the campaign, 24 million signatures had been gathered for the Jubilee 2000 petition, the first-ever global petition. World leaders had committed to writing off 100 billion dollars of debts owed by poor countries. Many people went on campaigning for further debt cancellations through organisations such as 'Jubilee Debt Campaign' (website www.jubileedebtcampaign.org. uk). In 2002 Bono established DATA (Debt Aids Trade Africa – website www.data.org), whose aim was to raise awareness about the crises swamping Africa. Bono also continued to support other charities and in an interview on the American TV channel CNN he was asked, 'What do you prefer doing, good works or making music?'

He replied: 'I'd much rather be in a rehearsal room or studio making rock'n'roll than dressing up in a suit and tie and representing the World Health Organisation. I think I'm better at it, I think I'm better suited to it. But you

Bono lobbying a USA senator in Washington in 2002

Photo by Ron Sachs/Rex Features

know what – they asked me here and I'm proud of the work I've done over the past few years on the debt campaign. And if they need a voice, they've got mine.'

Using money for debt repayment rather than being able to spend it on health has without doubt aggravated the problem of AIDS/HIV in poorer parts of the world. Approximately 25 million people in Sub-Saharan Africa are likely to die of the disease by 2012, leaving a whole generation of orphans - possibly as many as 40 million. Medication and education could prevent the disaster developing on such a frightening scale but it would be very costly.

In April 2002, Bono, a regular visitor to the White House, met with President Bush for half an hour to discuss the problem of AIDS in Africa. He said that as a rock star there were more glamorous things he could be doing rather than waiting in corridors to talk to politicians, however he felt it was worth talking to people who were in a position to make a real difference. He admitted that he may come across as a pest: 'I am a pest. I am a stone in the shoe of a lot of people living in this town ... But actually the President said, "That's what we need, come back ... keep at me." And I intend to.' In a press conference after the meeting, standing next to Bono, President Bush announced that America would be sending 5 billion dollars

Photo by Ron Sachs/Rex Features

Bono at a children's home in South Africa during a visit to promote AIDS awareness

Bono has also spoken to the general public when receiving many different awards, and continually over the years to thousands of fans world-wide at his concerts. He grabs any and every opportunity to use his fame to make a difference to the world. In 2002 he was voted by readers of *Q* magazine as the most powerful figure in the music industry, and in 2005 named 'Person of the Year' by *Time* magazine in the USA.

in grants to Africa. Bono was pleased with the decision but still hoped for more, admitting it was a start but it wasn't enough.

In September 2002 Bono went live on the prime-time American chat show 'Oprah'. In front of an audience of around 20 million Americans he described the problems of the AIDS victims in Africa. When he was asked why Americans should be concerned he said, 'Because every mother knows that the pain of losing a child is the same in Africa as it is in America.'

Few people have the opportunity to talk to such diverse groups as Bono. His desire for a more just world has seen him addressing politicians, heads of state and the United Nations Assembly. In September 2004 he addressed the UK Labour Party Conference, calling on the Government to 'Make Poverty History'. This campaign for increased aid, debt relief and trade justice (www.makepovertyhistory.org) gained huge international publicity through the global Live8 concerts in July 2005. These concerts were organised by Bono and Sir Bob Geldoff and held to coincide with a G8 summit in Scotland. This was a meeting of the leaders of the world's richest countries and Bono and Bob Geldoff spoke to them of their hopes of making poverty history. The summit made significant pledges in pursuit of this goal.

What Do You Think?

1. In what ways do you think people in rich countries may have responsibility for people in poorer countries?

2. What point was Bono making when he said: 'Because every mother knows that the pain of losing a child is the same in Africa as it is in America'?

3. Imagine you are in a band and have just received a Grammy award. What would you say in your acceptance speech? What do you think Bono would say?

4. Who would you vote as the most powerful person in the music industry today and why? How do they use their power?

Walk On

After the Jubilee 2000 campaign U2 released the album *All That You Can't Leave Behind*. It was appreciated by many world-wide as it raced to number one.

Many of the songs on the album dealt with difficult or emotive issues. *Stuck in a Moment* was written after the death of Bono's friend Michael Hutchence, singer in the band INXS, who is generally believed to have committed suicide. *Walk On* was dedicated to Aung San Suu Kyi, leader of the struggle against a brutal and oppressive regime in Burma (Myanmar). This Burmese woman had chosen to stay in Burma to challenge the government there. As a consequence she spent many years under house arrest, separated from her English husband and two sons. In 1991 she was awarded the Nobel Peace Prize.

Beautiful Day, on the same album, was released as a single and reached number one in charts all around the world. In the 2001 Grammy Awards the song won each of the three categories in which it had been nominated, including 'Song of the Year'. It seems to have an irrepressible feel-good impact that has resulted in it being used in a wide range of contexts, including theme tune for an ITV football programme. One of the inspirations for the song came from Bono's involvement in the Jubilee 2000 campaign when he finally believed that some of the world debt would be cancelled.

Their next album, *How to Dismantle an Atomic Bomb*, again topped the charts across the world. '... Bomb' is a personal collection of songs, expressing strong beliefs and feelings. *Vertigo* has Bono reflecting on the problems of being put on a pedestal. *Sometimes You Can't Make It On Your Own* shows Bono's heartfelt grief over the death of his father. He also ponders the meaning of death later on the album, in the track *One Step Closer*. The songs *Miracle Drug* and *Crumbs from Your Table* are about the AIDS crisis, calling on people not to judge others but to be more understanding and to do all they can to help those suffering.

The final track, *Yahweh* (the Hebrew word for God), seems like a personal prayer, with Bono offering himself for God's work: 'Take these hands don't make a fist ... Take this soul and make it sing...'. The song ends with the idea that no one can own Jerusalem and seems to call for respect between the faiths that view the city as sacred. In recent concerts Bono has worn a headband with 'COEXIST' on it. The 'C' has been drawn as a crescent, the 'X' as the Star of David and the 'T' as a cross.

The final words of *Yahweh* are: 'Take this heart and make it break'. Perhaps these suggest that after years of fame and political campaigning Bono still cares deeply about what is going on in the world.

What Do You Think?

1. Aung San Suu Kyi inspired Bono. Who would inspire you to action? Why?

2. What message do you think Bono was trying to convey through his headband? Have you ever worn anything that reflects your views? Is there anything you feel strongly enough about to declare on a T-shirt or wristband? Give reasons.

3. From what you have read, what would you say are the dominant issues and emotions in Bono's life?

4. What important challenges do you think will face Bono in the future?

Biographical Notes

10 May 1960 Paul Hewson born in Dublin.

10 September 1974 Paul's mother dies suddenly.

Summer 1976 Band members get together for the first time.

September 1979 Their debut record is released, entitled *U2-3*.

August 1982 Bono marries Alison Stewart, whom he had met at school. They later had four children.

March 1983 U2 perform on 'Top of the Pops'.

December 1983 U2 voted 'Band of the Year' by the Rolling Stone writers' poll.

July 1985 U2 play at Live Aid.

Autumn 1986 Bono and Alison visit El Salvador and Nicaragua.

April 1987 U2 become third rock band to appear on the cover of *Time* Magazine.

February 1988 U2 release the *Rattle and Hum* movie.

March 1988 U2 win 'Best Vocal of the Year' and 'Best Album of the Year' at the Grammy Awards. They went on to win similar awards in later years.

October 1997 U2 play to a crowd of 45 000 people in war-torn Sarajevo.

September 1999 Bono meets the Pope on behalf of the Jubilee 2000 Campaign.

March 2000 U2 granted the Freedom of the City of Dublin.

February 2001 U2 awarded the 'Outstanding Contribution to Music Gong' at the Brit Awards.

April 2002 Bono meets President Bush, who promises grants to Africa for the HIV crisis.

November 2003 Bono and The Edge join Nelson Mandela and other stars, including Beyoncé, at a five-hour concert broadcast for World AIDS Awareness Day.

September 2004 Bono addresses the Labour Party Conference, calling on the Labour Government to support the campaign to 'Make Poverty History'.

July 2005 Bono, along with Sir Bob Geldoff, organises the global Live8 concerts coinciding with the G8 summit in Scotland.

December 2005 Bono named 'Time Person of The Year' by *Time* magazine in America.

Albums released by U2 are listed on page 23.

Things to Do

1 The name *Bono* was originally short for *Bono Vox*, which means 'good voice'. *Bono* just means 'good'. Does Bono deserve this title? Write arguments either for or against this **OR** hold a class debate.

2 Imagine you are producing a documentary on Bono's life. In groups, plan what you would include. You could use music, drama, video, written material, etc. What aspect of Bono's life would you choose to be the main focus of the programme?

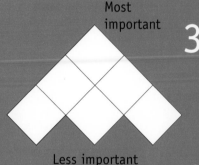

Most important

Less important

3 Think of six different aspects in Bono's life, e.g. money, family, politics, faith. Write them out and place them on a ranking grid in the order of priority that you think Bono might place them. The most important should be at the top of the pyramid, the next two together on the second level and three less important aspects at the bottom. Repeat the exercise only this time put them in the order of priority you would give them.

4 Write the 'back-cover blurb' for a book about Bono's life. Think about how you can make it appeal to as wide an audience as possible, not just his fans.

5 Find out about some new and different styles of church, e.g. café churches, churches in pubs, tribal generation, soul survivor, Greenbelt. (Some websites you could try are: www.soulsurvivor.com/uk or www.churchnext.net or www.clubberstemple.com or www.godweb.org or www.churchfortheunchurched.co.uk) Why do you think these new forms of churches may appeal to people who do not wish to attend more traditional churches?

6 Write out Psalm 70 (use the *Good News Bible* version if possible). Decide on the main emotions expressed by the writer of this Psalm. Choose a colour for each emotion. Now colour code the Psalm according to the feelings involved. This can be done by underlining the text in different colours, by changing the colour of the text or by highlighting different sections. Why do you think Bono and many other people find the Psalms helpful today?

7 Design a CD cover for one of U2's songs mentioned in this book. Try to bring out the different messages and issues contained in the lyrics.

8   In groups, prepare the lyrics of *Sunday Bloody Sunday* to be read as a poem. Decide how it will be read and where the emphasis should be put in order to communicate its message. (You could use the notes on the song on page 9 to help you.) Can you add movement or dance to make the message even clearer? Perform the reading then discuss or reflect on how your understanding of the song has developed as a result of the reading.

9   (a) Look at the lyrics or listen to a selection of U2 songs. Do you think any of them are protest songs? Can you think of any other musicians or bands who have sung protest songs? What issues were they protesting about?

(b) Try to find out what success these or other protest songs have had. Did they help bring about change? If so, how?

(c) Write a music review for one of U2's singles or a protest song of your choice. Look at the message of the lyrics and the music. Do they work together?

10   Imagine you are a solo artist. Design an album cover which contains a clue about what kind of beliefs and values you hold, just as U2 included 'J33-3' on their album *All You Can't Leave Behind*.

11   You are a U2 fan who has just been to one of their concerts. During the concert Bono spoke about the problem of the HIV/AIDS epidemic in Africa. Enact a telephone conversation with a friend telling them about the concert. Include as much detail about the situation in Africa as you can.

12   (a) The song *Grace* can be interpreted in a number of ways because 'grace' has several different meanings. Find the lyrics. What do you think the song is about? You may wish to use the notes on page 15.

(b) Listen to the song. Do you think the lyrics are a good match to the music? Why?/Why not?

13   Use the song *Grace* as a model for writing your own song or poem about something you feel deeply about.

14 Research **one** of the big political topics which Bono campaigned for, e.g. Northern Ireland, Jubilee 2000 or AIDS/HIV in Africa. Prepare a presentation to illustrate what Bono wanted to change, using appropriate U2 song lyrics when possible. Write a reflection on how you now see this issue.

15 (a) From the U2 website at www.U2.com find out about the most recent material that U2 have produced (try using the timeline). Look at the lyrics to any new songs. Do you recognise any familiar themes in their work? What new topics and themes can you find?

(b) Find the latest news on what Bono has been doing and saying. What links can you find between his actions, the new songs and his beliefs or values?

U2 have released the following albums to date:

Boy	October 1980	(highest chart position 52)
October	October 1981	(highest chart position 11)
War	March 1983	(highest chart position 1)
The Unforgettable Fire	October 1984	(highest chart position 1)
The Joshua Tree	March 1987	(highest chart position 1)
Rattle and Hum	October 1988	(highest chart position 1)
Achtung Baby	November 1991	(highest chart position 1)
Zooropa	July 1993	(highest chart position 1)
Pop	March 1997	(highest chart position 1)
All That You Can't Leave Behind	October 2000	(highest chart position 1)
How to Dismantle an Atomic Bomb	November 2004	(highest chart position 1)

Religious and Moral Education Press
A division of SCM-Canterbury Press Ltd
A wholly owned subsidiary of Hymns
Ancient & Modern Ltd
St Mary's Works, St Mary's Plain
Norwich, Norfolk NR3 3BH

First published 2004

Reprinted 2006

ISBN 1 85175 321 4

Designed and typeset by
TOPICS – The Creative Partnership,
Exeter

Printed in Great Britain by
Brightsea Press, Exeter for
SCM-Canterbury Press Ltd, Norwich

Notes for Teachers

The first Faith in Action books were published in the late 1970s and the series has remained popular with both teachers and pupils. However, much in education has changed over the last twenty years, such as the development of both new examination syllabuses in Religious Studies and local agreed syllabuses for Religious Education which place more emphasis on pupils' own understanding, interpretation and evaluation of religious belief and practice, rather than a simple knowledge of events. This has encouraged us to amend the style of the Faith in Action Series to make it more suitable for today's classroom.

The aim is, as before, to tell the stories of people who have lived and acted according to their faith, but we have included alongside the main story questions which will encourage pupils to think about the reasons for the behaviour of our main characters and to empathise with the situations in which they found themselves. We hope that pupils will also be able to relate some of the issues in the stories to other issues in modern society, either in their own area or on a global scale.

The 'What Do You Think?' questions may be used for group or class discussion or for short written exercises. The 'Things to Do' at the end of the story include ideas for longer activities for RE or Citizenship and offer opportunities for assessment.

In line with current syllabus requirements, as Britain is a multifaith society, Faith in Action characters are selected from a variety of faith backgrounds and many of the questions may be answered from the perspective of more than one faith.

Note Some questions in this book refer students to the U2 website www.U2.com However teachers are advised to check the U2 website **in advance** for suitability and for current availability of items such the lyrics of U2 songs.

Acknowledgements

The publishers would like to express their sincere thanks to Catherine Bowness for the invaluable work she did in developing the Faith in Action Series during her five years as Series Editor (1997–2002).

The author and publishers would also like to thank Margaret Cooling for her advice on questions and student tasks in this book.

This book has been published in association with The Stapleford Centre, The Old Lace Mill, Frederick Road, Stapleford, Nottingham NG9 8FN. Tel. 0115 939 6270. Website: www.stapleford-centre.org

Cover photo by RL/Keystone USA/Rex Features